CRYPTOCURRENCY

An Unofficial Guide

By

Stephen Blumenthal

COPYRIGHT NOTICE

Table Of Contents

Disclaimer

Any and all of the date given in this book is merely to be used for informational and educational purposes. It must not be used as basis for investment, financial or trading advice.

It does not suggest that you purchase any cryptocurrency or sell any cryptocurrency that you own. Nothing on this book should be taken as any offer to sell or buy any cryptocurrency.

As the purpose of this book is merely to provide information about cryptocurrency, you must do your own sufficient research from different sources and seek financial advice before making any decisions in investing in cryptocurrency.

This book strives to make sure that the information is accurate and correct, however, it cannot be held responsible for any inadequate, incomplete or incorrect information.

Understand that reading and using all of the information in this book would be at your own risk. The author of this book wrote it ONLY for information purposes and not for anything else.

If you DO choose to invest in, buy, sell or trade cryptocurrency, you would be doing it out of your own free will and not because of the information you have read in this book.

Introduction

Cryptocurrency is a relatively new concept to most people, but is rapidly gaining popularity. Simply put, it is a virtual form of money or currency which makes use of cryptography as safety measures.

Cryptocurrency is tough to counterfeit because of the cryptographic security feature. This security feature is made up of extremely intricate systems of code which encrypt sensitive data transfers in order to protect the exchange of units.

The developers of cryptocurrency have made these security features based on computer engineering and mathematical principles, making them enormously difficult, even impossible to crack.

Aside from that, the security features also hide the identity of their users so that transactions cannot be attributed to any specific person, group or organization.

A key feature of this kind of currency is its organic nature. It doesn't come from any central authority which means it cannot be manipulated by the government, in theory.

The worth and quantity of cryptocurrencies depend on the people or groups who use them. To be specific, the actions of the miners (we will be learning about miners further on) are vital to the constancy and effortless function of cryptocurrencies.

Aside from being organic, it is also anonymus in nature. This makes it quite popular for those who would like to perform disresputable activities, like tax evasion, money laundering and such. See, when dealing with fiat currency, the government can very easily freeze or take away a person's bank account as long as it is in their jurisdiction. But for cryptocurrency, on the other hand, it would be very difficult to get a hold of these funds, even if the owner is a citizen of the country.

It's important to note that cryptocurrencies can re traded in for "real money" in specific online markets. This means that each cryptocurrency has an exchange rate with the most common and major currencies of the world. However, these exchanges are quite prone to hacking, making them one of the most frequent places where digital theft occurs.

There is a finite supply of cryptocurrencies out there. The source codes of these currencies have their own commands which gives the exact number of units which can and will be able to exist. This means that as the years go by, miners would have much more difficulty producing units of cryptocurrency. Just like gold and precious stones and metals, cryptocurrencies are naturally prone to deflation.

Using this kind of currency comes with its own advantages and disadvantages, which will be discussed later on. Now let's learn about the origins of this modern currency.

The Origin of Cryptocurrency

Cryptocurrency has an extensive and profound origin. It's worth learning about it in case you are interested in investing in it. Without adequate knowledge, you won't know how to ask the right questions and look for the best solutions.

So let's learn about the origin of cryptocurrency...

In the Beginning

One of the first known efforts at inventing cryptocurrencies had happened in the Netherlands roughly in the 1980s. The need for these kinds of currencies had arisen because of some petrol stations.

Problems had arisen when these petrol stations in the more remote areas of the Netherlands were constantly being robbed of cash and the owners were not comfortable with the risk of placing security guards there. The problem was, the petrol stations had to stay in operation 24 hours a day so that trucks and vehicles of travelers have access to fuel no matter what time of the day or night.

It was then that someone had the brilliant idea to put money into "smartcards," which were being tested at that time, and so the first variation of electronic cash (or cryptocurrency) was used.

Instead of having to pay with cash, truck drivers were given these smartcards, making the petrol stations less susceptible to robbery.

At around that same time, one of the main retailers, by the name of Albert Heijn, was trying to convince banks in the area to come up with a way to permit shoppers to make payments straight from their bank accounts. In time, this had been refined to become what we now know as point-of-sale.

The Humble Beginnings of Digital Cash

Prior to all of this, an American cryptographer named David Chaum has already been exploring the possibility of what it would take to generate electronic cash.

He had various views on privacy and on the use of money which had pushed him to believe that there are safer ways of transaction. He thought that in order to ensure secure transactions, we would need a kind of currency that would be just like actual fiat currency, but with an added privcy feature.

At around the year 1983, he had come up with a blinding formula, which is still an existing addition to the algorithm which is still used in today's cryptocurrency encryption. This formula allows one user to give a particular number to another user which is to be modified by the receiver. Then, when the receiver deposits her coin (as Chaum named it) into a bank, it carries the original signature of the bank but a different number with which the bank is signed.

This invention permitted the "coin" to be altered undetected without breaking the signature of the bank so it remained "blind" to the transaction.

In the late 1980s, David Chaum has started DigiCash and continued on building his invention of Internet currency. This invention of "blinded cash" was amazing and it had been the cause of much attention from the press.

Sadly though, David Chaum (along with his entire company) had made some unwise decisions, which caused trouble with the central bank in the Netherlands. They had agreed that the products of DigiCash would only p be sold to banks and no one else. Through this deal, the company had tried to handle the digital cash to lots of banks, which in time had led to their bankruptcy in the year 1998.

The Emergence of Web Based Money

Following DigiCash were numerous startups which were working on the same thing.

In the mid 1990s, the focus moved from Europe to North America. However, the first wave of cryptocurrencies had failed but was quickly left behind by the second - and more enduring, wave of web based currency.

First Virtual was the first to emerge, but was immediately replaced by PayPal and they basically did the same thing. However, PayPal permitted the transfer of money from one person to another unlike First Virtual which required the users to become merchants first, which the majority of people disliked.

PayPal also allowed its system as being a hand-to-hand cash. The first versions of PayPal were available on the Palm Pilot, which was very popular with nerds. This focus on the "nerd market" was quickly discarded as PayPal found out that the majority of users really wanted currency on the web browser.

PayPal also discovered an enthusiastic userbase in the eBay market, so its future was basically ascertained as long as they made sure to evade the regulatory minefield which had been laid out for it.

PayPal had grown in popularity and had proven web as the protocol of choice, even for currency and transactions. Because of this, Chaum's earlier ideas were basically forgotten. As PayPal grew in popularity, a lot of other business etnterprises began pursuing a variation of it, which was gold on the web.

The first company to succeed was named e-gold. It was an operation based in America which had its main corporation in the Carribean. The idea behind e-gold was fairly simple - all you had to do was send them your gold and they would give your e-gold as credit in your account. You could do that or you can purchase e-gold from them, send a wire transfer and then they would use that to buy and take hold of the gold you paid for.

E-gold had quickly grown and hept on growing until the year 1999. Since the corporation was not in America, it did not need any approval from the US, which allowed it to aim for the American market comprised of people who were looking to buy gold. It had also catered to the expanding market of dealers who had the need to make payments across the border.

With the rapid increase in popularity, the self-sufficient exchange market gained more momentum in the year 2000 and it seemed like it was around to stay.

The Issure Regarding the Regulatory Bust

Prevalent as it was, e-gold unfortunately ran into difficulties because of its policy of allowing anyone and everyone who is interested to open an account. Because of this, a lot of scammers started signing up, which had caught the interest of the Feds.

The Feds then proceeded to raid the offices of e-gold in Florida, ending its reign. All the similar competitors the Feds could get their hands on were also removed, thus ending the second wave or web based currency.

When you think about it, the 9/11 incident played a big role in the story of cryptocurrency. Prior to the horrific incident, the USA was more liberal about alternative currencies like cryptocurrency. They used to view these as innovations and promising business. However, after the 9/11 incident cryptocurrencies were presumed to be a source of transactions for terrorists and other people interested in illegal, dangerous activities.

As this was happening in America, what was happening in Europe was a different story. They had seen that the efforts to totally get rid of cryptocurrencies was going very well. Because of this,

Internet businesses had made the decision to set up base in America.

Fast forward to 2008, the most widely used cryptocurrency now, Bitcoin was brought to the public by Satoshi Nakamoto and since then, different kinds of cryptocurrencies have emerged, gaining more and more users. Now it looks as if cryptocurrencies are becoming a trend and more and more people are getting interested.

How Does It Work?

True enough, cryptocurrency does have a lengthy history and it has come a long way from how it started out to how it is presented and used in these modern times. But in reality, does everyone know how cryptocurrency works?

How do miners (yes, we will be explaining what miners are further on) actually make the coins and how are transactions created and verified?

To be able to have a clearer idea of how it works, it would be helpful to analyze the mechanizm which controls the databases of cryptocurrencies. Cryptocurrencies are made up of a network of people. Each and every person then has a documentation of the whole history of all the transactions he has made as well as the balance of every account.

Let's have an example.

A transaction would be a file indicating that person 1 gave a number of coins to person 2, then it is signed by the private key of person 1. Basically it makes use of public key cryptography. After the transaction has been signed, it is then transmitted to all the other people in the network.

The whole network of people is then informed of the transaction but it is only confirmed after a specified amount of time. It would be good to note that confirmation is a vital part of cryptocurrency. In fact, you can say that cryptocurrency is all about confirmation.

You see, if the transaction isn't confirmed, it remains in a pending status, making it prone to being forged. As soon as a transaction has been confirmed, it is already permanent. It can't be forged, it cannot be undone and it has already been documented in the transaction record of the so-called blockchain.

This is where miners come in. The job of the miners is to confirm transactions in a network of cryptocurrencies, and only they are able to do this. What they do is they accept the transactions, verify them as legitimate then share them in the network. After a miner has confirmed a transaction, it has to be added to the database, therefore making it part of the blockchain.

As a reward for doing their job, miners are given tokens of the cryptocurrency as compensation. So you can see how valuable miners are to the whole concept of cryptocurrency.

Because of this, it would be relevant to take a more profound look at what miners are actually doing. Delve into the details of their work and how they keep cryptocurrencies going.

The fact is, anyone can be a miner. As the network is decentralized it has no power to assign tasks, so the cryptocurrency needs a kind of procedure to avoid a ruling party from misusing it. For instance, without this procedure, a person would be able to create a multitude of persons to scatter forged trnsaction, therefore destroying the system.

To solve this issue, a rule has been made stating that miners would have to devote work of their computers to be eligible for the task. To do this, they would have to discover a product of a cryptographic function which links up the new block with its precursor. Being able to do this is called the Proof-of-Work and would qualify you to be a miner.

To put it in more comprehensible terms, miners would have to find the solution to a cryptologic puzzle. As soon as the miner solves the puzzle, he can build his own block and attach it to the blockchain. As a reward, the miner is given the privelage to add a coinbase transaction, which then gives him an amount of cryptocurrency. This is basically how cryptocurrency is created and how it works.

The Properties of Cryptocurrency

Cryptocurrency has different properties which set them apart from other kinds of currencies. There are three major properties of cryptocurrency that would be important to learn about.

The Revolutionary Properties

Cryptocurrencies are basically entries in a decentralized consensus database. The reason for the name is that the security of the whole process is ensured because of efficient cryptography features. The security of cryptocurrencies depends on logic and math rather than on trust and on people.

When explaining the properties of cryptocurrencies, we need to differentiate the transactional and monetary properties, which have significant differences.

The Transactional Properties

- Cryptocurrencies are Irreversible
  When your transaction has been confirmed, you won't be able to reverse the process. This means that NOBODY can aid you in taking back the money you had sent. If you send an amount to someone and that someone turns out to be a hacker or a scammer, you'd have no way to get it back once the transaction has been confirmed. So very careful in making transactions.
- Cryptocurrencies ande Pseudonymous
  Transactions and accounts are never connected to "real world identities." The addresses in which you receive your cryptocurrencies from are not actual addresses but random ones.

- Cryptocurrencies are Quick and Available Around the Globe
  Since transactions are made online, they are immediately sent to the network and within a few minutes, they can be confirmed and would already be permanent. Being online, these transactions and cryptocurrencies are available to anyone anywhere in the world.
- Cryptocurrencies are Secure
  As previously stated, cryptocurrencies are secured in a key cryptography system. Cryptocurrency by the owner of the private key when he decides to send it.
- Cryptocurrencies Can Be Used Without Permission
  To be able to make use of cryptocurrency, you don't have to ask permission from anyone. All you have to do is download software or sign up and start using it!

The Monetary Properties

- The Supply of Cryptocurrency is Controlled
  There is a limit to the supply of tokens for most of the cryptocurrencies out there. The supply of cryptocurrencies is controlled by a schedule which is written in the code. This means that the stock of a cryptocurrency in the future can be estimated even by today.
- There is No Debt
  Unlike fiat currency in your bank, which is created through an IOU system, cryptocurrencies do not correspond to any

debts. They are a concrete representation of themselves. What you see on your account is what you actually own.

Cryptocurrencies are truly revolutionary. As long as you take the time to understand the properties of cryptocurrency, then you will have a more profound comprehension of what it is all about.

The Difference Between Money and Cryptocurrency

Of course we all know what money (also known as fiat money) is. It's either paper or coins which we use to pay for goods, merchandise or services. There are different kinds of fiat money all over the world, depending on the country of origin.

On the other hand, cryptocurrency is merely a form of electronic money. They come in the form of "tokens" or "coins," to which values are assigned. These values make them worth real or fiat money.

Right now, there are more than 600 cryptocurrencies available in the market. They are similar to regular currency but the difference is they make use of cryptographic security features to make sure that they are unchangeable and we are sure of their source. The cryptography security feature also allows for secure transfer and storage of information which is sensitive.

Unlike fiat money, which mainly moves through banking systems, cryptocurrencies work with mathematics and complicated computer encryption. Also unlike fiat money or gold reserves, cryptocurrency isn't supported by the country's central bank. Instead it is disseminated by a community of users.

Because of this, users have more freedom and are able to take control of their own money, without interference from the government. Owning cryptocurrency doesn't mean you are bound by any type of service agreement, allowing you to get more out of your money for a longer period of time.

Cryptocurrency was intended to as currency for enrichment of wealth as these kinds of currency are basically limited. This is when the supply and demand aspect of economics come into play. This means that as a more users begin utilizing a specific cryptocurrency, the demand for it increases. However, because they are limited, they become lesser. As this happens, the price of the currency increases as well and as long as the demand is high, the price will continue to increase. This makes it more similar to goods rather than to currency.

As a matter of fact, the use of cryptocurrency is less expensive than the use of regular currency since there are no "middle-men" involved, which is usually in thw form of the bank. Cryptocurrecy can be sent straight to anyone around the world and can be confirmed then received in a matter of minutes. The traditional banking system, which employs verification and clearing processes takes much longer, usually days rather than mere minutes.

Aside from that, the fee for transfer is minimal compared to transferring regular money through the bank. Any amount of cryptocurrency can be transferred through the web and the fee wouldn't be felt much. With this, the government cannot interfere with your account since it works with a decentralized system.

Another feature of the cryptocurrency is the blockchain technology. This is a ground-breaking clear system which was made along with the very first digital currency in the world in the year 2009. The blockchain is a public ledger which documents each and every transaction, whether sending or receiving cryptocurrency, that happens between users in real time.

Anyone and everyone has access to these transactions and can see them anytime. This key feature is what permits cryptocurrency to be decentralized and this is what other kinds of cryptocurrencies stem from.

Why Use Cryptocurrency Instead of Money?

As previously stated, there are hundreds of kinds of cryptocurrencies available in the market today, so it would be very helpful to start learning everything you can about this new kind of currency. No two kinds of cryptocurrency is alike but thay all provide the same kinds of benefits.

Also as stated earlier, cryptocurrencies aren't directly connected to any government rules, regulations or laws, nor are they linked to any banks or corporations. Therefore, you won't have to pay any fees, charges and rates such as those you have to pay for your credit card or bank. Aside from that, cryptocurrency isn't affected by inflation rates, therefore not affecting their value.

Users of cryptocurrency also enjoy the benefits of anonymity. In making transactions with fiat currency through the bank, credit cards or even ATMs, you'd have to give your personal information along with other data to help confirm your identity. This makes it easier for the bank, other businesses or even the government to track your every move as well as all your transactions. In dealing with cryptocurrency, you don't have to surrender all of this information, giving you more privacy.

Finally, having an account with regular currency would make you prone to government interferance. They would have the power and authority to seize or freeze your account, rendering you unable to access it. This cannot be done with cryptocurrency accounts, which makes it have more appeal to users, especially the ones who plan to do suspicious or illegal activity.

What You Need to Know Before Using Cryptocurrency

Before you even begin thinking about investing in and using cryptocurrency, there are a few relevant things you'd have to know. By now you've probably seen how popular cryptocurrencies have become and how more and more people have opted to start using them. This would have possibly peaked your interest and that is why you are trying to get as much knowledge and information as you can about it.

It is important to be wary of cryptocurrency, just as any online transactions because of their lack of rules and regulations. They are designed to be outside of the control of the government to give users more freedom, which can also be part of why you should be more cautious when dealing with them.

Cryptocurrencies are a very significant concept. It is an extremely new and innovative way for people around the world to be able to make transactions while keeping track of their accounts online. Though despite increasing value and demand of cryptocurrency, it would also be important to note that a lot of people have already lost a lot on them.

So before you go into cryptocurrency, here are a few important things to know about them:

- **Think of it as a Consideration and not as an Investment**
  To be very clear, it is obvious that cryptocurrencies have a dazzling future as a brand new way to perform commerce. But that doesn't mean that their current usefulness will permanently last.
  When you think about it, cryptocurrency is still in its early days of developing and even though it is becoming increasingly popular, it still isn't enough to be established as a justifiable trade. This means that you should be looking at it as merely a consideration or a speculation rather than an actual investment.

Take this direction unless you are planning to immediately spend all your cryptocurrency or you are just planning to accumulate all you can and store them until they become more sustainable.

- **Avoid Placing All Your Money or Your Savings on Cryptocurrency**
Nowadays the value of cryptocurrency is susceptible to the current trends set by new users (much like you, if you choose to start using them) and the users who have been using them for a while now, but are waiting for their chance to get out of the market.
This makes the stability of the cryptocurrency market uncertain at this point but that doesn't mean it's a lost cause. You can still be able to make money in the long term as long as you do your research and make smart decisions.
So again, be very careful and don't put all your eggs in one basket, as they say. Staking all your life savings into cryptocurrency might not be the best choice right now.
It would be smarter to start with smaller amounts rather than going big. Just like any endeavour, testing the waters first would be more ideal. You'd also be in a better position to monitor the market without worrying that you'll be losing everything you have.

- **Paranoia Will Be Helpful in This Situation**
While some see investing in cryptocurrency as profitable, others also see it as an opportunity

to rob other people who haven't been cautious enough about the safety of their online wallets. The anonymity comes as an advantage to these kinds of people since they won't be caught easily.

To be able to ensure the safety of your cryptocurrency, again you'd have to do a lot of research and try to find out which kinds offet the best security features. Look for the most reputable ones and even if you've found those ones, doing more research on them would be smart.

When setting up your account, make sure your passwords are strong and go for two-factor authentications or more, if available. In the case of cryptocurrency, being paranoid about security will really help you out rather than hinder you.

- **You'd Need a Strong Resolve to Invest in Cryptocurrency**

One of the most vital things to have before starting to buy and use cryptocurrency is a strong stomach and the knowledge to know that you shouldn't invest any money you are not prepared to lose. This doesn't mean that you will surely lose the money, but you should be prepared of that possibility.

One of the poorest characteristics of bad traders is their failure to hang around when the market drops. They only make their purchases when the market is up, then panic and sell everything once the market goes down. This is not a good strategy, but it is common with beginners.

Now if you think of the money you put into cryptocurrency as "already lost," but keep on working with it, you'd be better off. You'd be making better decisions as you're monitoring the market, so when it spikes or drops, you don't panic. In fact, you can actually profit from those who are panic selling as you can buy out their assets for a lower value.

It would also be clever to monitor different cryptocurrencies for you to be able to see which are more stable compared to the others. Also, when you do this, you'd have a higher chance of turning a profit and you'd be influencing the market as well.

- **It Cannot be Reiterated Enough - BE CAREFUL**

To be able to profit from cryptocurrencies and make money off of them, you have to be careful, smart and willing to take advantage of the movements in the market. Also, don't make this your only job - continue on with your day job and stay smart when buying, selling, using and generally trading cryptocurrencies.

The cryptocurrency market is constantly dipping and spiking so you should also be constantly keeping track of it.

When you think about it, the value of cryptocurrencies actually increases when the number of users increase as well. When users utilize cryptocurrencies to make purchases, the demand increases and their worth as well. This then pushes companies, corporations and organizations to accept cryptocurrency as a means of transactions.

Considering cryptocurrencies would give you an upperhand as you'd already be included in the market and you'd have the potential to make money once it grows. However, it would be good to keep in mind that this is in no way a get-rich-quick scheme. Always be careful, smart and responsible when getting into cryptocurrency, just as any decisions you make in life.

The Uses of Cryptocurrency

Just like regular currency, cryptocurrency can be used in a variety of different ways. It may be a lot newer than regular money but it's quite easy to learn how to use it. Who knows, once you learn all the different uses of cryptocurrency, you'd be itching to find the best one and sign up for your own account.

But don't rush off just yet, we still have a long way to go as we are still at the earlier part of your overall learning. First let's examine the many uses of cryptocurrency so you would have a better idea, should you choose to start using it.

- **Use Cryptocurrency to Make a Donation**
  If you are fond of making donations, this particular use of cryptocurrency would probably interest you. When you aremaking a donation, are you absolutely sure that the whole

amount goes to the cause or charity you inteded to give it to? Or are you worried that a percentage of the amount - however small or big, goes elsewhere? Eliminate the need for solicitation services and directly transfer the amount you want to the charity of your choice. Since cryptocurrency has a P2P sharing feature, which is unique to it, you can rest easy and know that your money will reach the charity or cause you wanted your donation to go to.

- **Purchase an Outstanding Cup of Coffee or Something Equally Satisfying**
  Business owners have started accepting cryptocurrency as a means for payment of customers. Cafes, restaurants and even online shops have joined the bandwagon and opted for change and advancement. The next time you enter a cafe or a shop, ask the staff if they accept payments through cryptocurrency and start using your money for practical things.

- **Use Your Cryptocurrency to Travel the World**
  Have you always dreamed of travelling the world? If you have a ready supply of cryptocurrency, go ahead and search for sites where you can book tickets and make payments using it. Allow yourself freedom to explore new places and try new things simply by going online and completing your transactions with your cryptocurrency.

- **Look into Buying or Selling Art**

There are certain sites, such as Bitpremier.com which provide a market for people to buy and sell art pieces and other luxury merchandise. The great thing about these kinds of sites it you can perform transactions using cryptocurrency, which is very convenient if you own some.

- **Further Your Education**
  Some schools have chosen the path of change and innovation by accepting cryptocurrency as a method of payment for tuition fees. The very first accredited school to do this is located in Cyprus, the University of Nicosia. Aside from accepting cryptocurrency as payment, they also offer a Masters Degree with a major in Digital Currency, which can be quite interesting and beneficial.

- **Be a Homeowner**
  Thinking of buying yourself a home or a property? There are lots of options online - and now you can purchase a house or lot with the use of cryptocurrency. All you need to do is research for sites or real estate agencies which accept cryptocurrency and you're all set!

- **Get a New Ride**
  Not ready for a house? Then maybe you're more interested un buying yourself a brand new car. Cars can now be purchased using cryptocurrency as well. Again, you'd have to find dealers which accept this form of currency so you can bring your dream car home with you.

- **Contribute to Crown Funding**

You've probably already heard of Kickstarter - the company which uses crowd funding to raise enough money for the purpose of allowing someone to complete his/her project. If you are interested in a particular person's project or proposal, you can make a donation to help make it happen. Nowadays, there are other companies - such as Lighthouse which have built their platforms for crowdfunding using cryptocurrency. The same process is followed, the cryptocurrency is stored until the amount reaches the desired amount of the project, before it is given to the person who has proposed the project itself.

In crowd funding, you have the option to retrieve your donation as long as the campaign hasn't been completed yet. All you have to do is inform the company that you'd like to pull out your donation.

- **Have an Opportunity to Go to Outerspace**
  Virgin Galactic, a company owned by Richard Branson, who is an enthusiastic supporter of cryptocurrency accepts it as payment for a chance to go into space. There are also some cryptocurrencies, such as MarsCoin which have claimed that this particular currency should be the official currency in Mars when we make it there.

- **Share Your Wealth**
  If you've started using cryptocurrency and you've actually seen and experienced their

benefits, why no share some to your friends to encourage them to join the market and add to the many users who have already invested in cryptocurrency.

- **Spend Your Money in Private**
  Sometimes you would want or even need to make discreet purchases for one reason or another. The privacy feature of different cryptocurrencies allows you to do this. Since all purchases and transactions are anonymus, you can freely proceed to make transactions whenever you wish without fear of being known.

- **Transfer Money Sans the High Fees**
  If you need to transfer money - whether locally or internationally, you can do so using cryptocurrency. The great thing about it is you won't be charged (or at least you won't be charged much) for the transfer and as an added bonus, your receipient will obtain the currency in a matter of minutes!

- **Do Your Grocery Shopping with Cryptocurrency**
  As an added convenience for online shoppers, a number of online grocers have accepted cryptocurrency as a mode of payment. This is very convenient especially if you have cryptocurrency and you prefer to do your grocery shopping online rather than having to actually go to supermarkets which cost more time, effort and money.

As you can see, though cryptocurrency hasn't been established enough to replace credit and debit cards, it still has a lot of uses. From common ways to use them to more unique ways (such as going into space!), cryptocurrency is slowly starting to place itself as a part of everyday life.

Since one of the main purposes of cryptocurrency is to simplify and speed up financial transactions, the fact that more businesses are adapting cryptocurrency is very helpful. If more businesses accept cryptocurrency, the number of interested people will increase and when those people actually sign up for cryptocurrency, then the number of users will also increase. This could cause a snowball effect wherein cryptocurrency continues to grow in terms of awareness and popularity until it takes over the majority of the population.

This, of course, is only a possibility. Right now you can just take comfort in the fact that cryptocurrency actually has a lot of uses and that's why it is gaining momentum.

All About Cryptocurrency

Are you starting to get a clearer picture about cryptocurrency? One thing you would have probably realized by now is that it is in now way a simple concept. Cryptocurrency comes with a lot of information and consideration in order for someone to really, profoundly understand it.

Read on to learn more about how to buy and use it, a few of the most popular examples of it and a few of the most common terms you'd be encountering when dealing with it.

How to Buy and Use Cryptocurrency

You are now aware of the instability of the cryptocurrecny market and how rates and values can easily fluctuate in even the shortest amounts of time. Now let's go into learning how one can purchase and use cryptocurrency.

When you purchase or are given cryptocurrency, along with it you also receive a digital key and an address where you can gain access to that currency. You can make use of that key to gain access, validate or even approve transactions.

To be able to keep your key secure, you will also be given a cryptocurrency wallet. These wallets can come in different varieties and all you have to do is choose which one would suit you the best or which one would you be most comfortable using. Here are the different varieties of cryptocurrency wallets which are available:

I. **A Desktop Wallet**

    If you prefer a desktop wallet, you'd have to download and install a software (such as Cryptonator) on your desktop. This would then permit you to send and store your cryptocurrency addresses. This wallet also allows you to link to the nework and keep track of all your transactions.

II. **An Online Wallet**

    Having an online wallet would mean that your cryptocurrency keys would be stored online through the use of exchange platforms. An online wallet would allow you to access your keys from anywhere, which may be convenient for some users. Some examples of these would be Circle and Coinbase.

III. **A Paper Wallet**

    A few of the sites sometimes allow you to choose a paper wallet service. You would then be able to create a piece of paper with 2 QR codes written on it. The first code is the public address where you are able to receive your cryptocurrencies. The second code is the private address which you can use for spending your cryptocurrency.

IV. **A Hardware Wallet**

    This option would give you a USB device which would be purposely made to store your cryptocurrency electronically along with your private address keys.

Easy, isn't it? Buying and using cryptocurrency is not that complicated but it doesn't only involve that. There are a lot more things to learn about to be able to efficiently deal with cryptocurrency.

Some Examples of Cryptocurrency

In order to give you an even better picture of the kinds of cryptocurrency, let's take a look at the most popular and most widely used kinds of cryptocurrencies which are currently available in the market now.

Knowing these would at least give you an idea on what cryptocurrencies are out there and which ones you can start researching on more.

- **Bitcoin**
  The very first and most well known cryptocurrency. Even if you haven't started using cryptocurrency, you've probably already heard of this. Bitcoin acts as the digital standard for gold in the entire industry of cryptocurrency. It is widely used as a global method of payment and is the actual currency used in most cyber crimes such as in ransomware or in the darknet market.
  Since it was released in 2009, the price of Bitcoin has then gone up from zero to more than $650 million. The volume of transactions has already reached more than 200,000

transactions on a daily basis. Because of this, it looks like Bitcoin has good sustainability.

- **Ethereum**
  Created by Vitalik Buterin, a crypto-genius, this kind of cryptocurrency has rapidly grown in popularity, second to Bitcoin.
  It has a blockchain technology is able to balance and validate accounts and process transactions but it is also able to process intricate programs and contracts as well.
  There are different versions of Ethereum, thus making it more of a group of currencies rather than an individual kind of currency.

- **Litecoin**
  Litecoin happens to be one of the first cryptocurrencies that was created after Bitcoin. It is known as the "silver" to the "digital gold" Bitcoin.
  This is much quicker, has a bigger quantity of tokens and has a newer mining algorithm. This innovation had seemed to be perfectly customized to be like a smaller version of Bitcoin. Through it, or rather through the basecode used in it, other similar cryptocurrencies (such as Feathercoin and Dogecoin) came into being.
  Though it has lost its second place standing after Bitcoin, it is still being actively cultivated and users still use it for trading now.

- **Monero**
  Monero is probable the best model which makes use of the cryptonite algorithm, which

was created to add some useful features in terms of privacy.

Unlike with Bitcoin and other cryptocurrencies where each transaction is recorded in the blockchain technology, Monero had a feature known as ring-signatures. This is the cryptonite algorithm which severed the trail of transaction records, granting users a higher degree of privacy.

In the year 2016, Monero reached its peak because the darknet markets made the decision to use it as their currency. Because of this, the price had gone higher, however, the actual utilization of this particular cryptocurrency remains lesser.

- **Blackcoin**

  To be able to verify a Blackcoin block, the user must stake a number of coins from their own waller as PoS. Coins are spent if the block isn't confirmed.

  In Blackcoins, the mining process is a lot faster and it doesn't consume as much power.

- **Dash**

  Anonymity is the main feature of this kind of cryptocurrency as it makes use of "Masternodes" in completing transactions. Wish Dash, it is difficult, if not impossible for other users to view your savings or any of your transactions as it doesn't have a public ledger.

- **Dogecoin**

  The Hash Algorithm Scrypt was created through this particular cryptocurrency. This was supposed to avoid the monopolization of mining by a single person or huge organizations.

Though the system didn't actually work, a lot of people still choose to use Dogecoin.

- **Peercoin**

  This cryptocurrency is different from others as it has a PoS / PoW fusion feature. There is no bound on the number of coins mined however it was created to ultimately get an inflation rate of 1%

- **Ripple**

  However less popular (some even say this is the most hated one), it would be helpful to learn about this particular kind of cryptocurrency too.

  While Ripple has its own local cryptocurrency (which is the XRP), it is more like a network which is used to process IOUs rather than the actual cryptocurrency itself.

  The local currency doesn't actually work as a means to store and exchange value but more as something for the network to use as protection from spam.

  Because of this, users don't consider Ripple as a real cryptocurrency as it doesn't have respectable store value.

Aside from these most well-known cryptocurrencies, there are hundreds more. Some are more reputable than others while some are merely attempts to make a quick buck or to get the attention of investors.

Again, be sure to do enough research on the kinds of cryptocurrencies before deciding on which to go with. We will be talking about other kinds further on so keep on reading!

Some Useful Terms You May Encounter

To be able to gain a full understanding of cryptocurrency and everything it comprises, it would also be useful to learn the most common terms used when dealing with it. To avoid confusion and to be able to keep up with the trend, you need to have an idea of these terms and what they mean.

Being able to understand technical terms in any concept is useful, and learning about cryptocurrency is no different. Build your cryptocurrency knowledge bank by familiarizing yourself with these terminologies.

1. 51% Attack
This is the name given to a condition wherein more than 50% of the computing authority in a network is controlled by just one person or a single group. This authority then gives them full and total rule over the network.

2. Address
This is the location where you would hold, send or receive your cryptocurrency. On the other hand, a wallet address is the public part of the keys needed for you to go through with your transactions.

3. Altcoin

This is the most accepted name for any cryptocurrency which isn't Bitcoin.

4. ASIC or ASIC Miner

ASIC (which means application-specific integrated circuit) mining is a cunning way to mine different coins at a quicker rate. An ASIC is basically a chip which is purposely made for mining. So an ASIC miner is someone who works on mining using this chip.

5. Blockchain

Already mentioned a couple of times in this book, a blockchain is a data system which permits the formation of a documentation of all the transactions made in a network which isn't centralized.

Through cryptography, people and computers around the globe are able to work together to be able to design a network as opposed to a network being designed or created by a single person or group. As a plus, the network is also protected by the cryptography.

Now the blockchain is made up of blocks made by people and it constantly grows as each block is created. Another feature of a blockchain is that it can be seen by everyone.

6. Block

These are files in a digital documentation. Data on these blocks cannot be modified and they are permanently stored once they are verified.

7. Block Height

This refers to the quantity of blocks following the first block in a blockchain.

8. Block Reward

This is the incentive given to a miner when he/she is able to successfully hash or solve a mathematical problem in regards to a block.

9. Central and Distributed Ledger

A central ledger is a written arrangement of synchronized data which is replicable but is managed by a single person or network.

A distributed ledger is a written arrangement of shared, synchronized data which can be replicated and therefore spread throughout different networks through different computers.

10. Fork

This refers to the enduring deviation of a different working version of the blockchain. These usually emerge when there is a 51% attack, a bug is found in the program or new rules would surface.

11. Halving

This is the decrease of minable rewards after a certain number of blocks have been created.

12. Hashrate

This refers to the rate at which a block is uncovered as well as the rate at which a mathematical problem which is related to it is solved.

13. Mining

This refers to the process of discovering and solving blocks on a blockchain.

14. Multisig

This refers to a form of security wherein there is more than just one signature to grant a transaction and this is very useful in business setting.

15. Node

This is basically a computer which is linked to the network. It serves as a support for the network through the process of relaying and validating transactions while being able to obtain a duplicate of the entire blockchain.

16. P2P

A shortcut of the term peer-to-peer. Interactions in a blockchain can be done through P2P.

17. PoW

This means Proof of Work. It was originally created to prevent DDOS attacks and spam emails. This is basically date which is extremely expensive to make however it can be easily confirmed by another party.

18. PoS

This means Proos of Stake. It is considered as the better substitute for PoW. The difference is that this system demands to be shown evidence of ownership of a certain amount of money.

19. Public and Private Key

This is a term used in cryptography and it refers to the key which can be used to encrypt and decode a message.

20. Signature

This is a mathematical equation which is used to test someone to prove that they, in fact, own the data, wallet or such.

21. Smart Contract

This is an agreement kept within a blockchain which cannot be modified. It has specific operations based on logic and is similar to written contracts.

These are the most common terminologies you would be able to encounter when dealing with cryptocurrency. Now that you know them, you would be more familiar when you decide to start using them.

The Advantages of Using Cryptocurrencies

Cryptocurrency is quickly gaining momentum in the market and for a good reason. There are several advantages of using cryptocurrency. If you're already using credit or debit cards, whether online or otherwise, it means you've already started using tools for digital currency.

So making use of cryptocurrency wouldn't be such a big leap. Read on to learn about the many advantages of using cryptocurrency.

- **Minimal Fees for Transaction**
  Since miners (who work to create cryptocurrency) are already paid with cryptocurrency straight from the network, you don't have to worry about being asked for fees or surcharges for your transactions.
- **Sole Ownership**
  Only you would be able to have access to your own currency as long as you keep your digital key safe and secure. Also, your account cannot be seized or frozen by anyone.
- **Your Identity Remains Secure**
  While using credit or debit cards require you to give out your personal information, cryptocurrency doesn't. You are allowed to just send any amount money without having to give away your identity.

- **Very Easy Access**
  Since cryptocurrency can be accessed from any computer with an internet connection, it means you would have access to your funds wherever you are and whenever you want.
- **No Risk - for Sellers**
  When cryptocurrency payments are sent and confirmed, there is no way to reverse them. This gives sellers an edge as the payments cannot be stopped, meaning you won't be defrauded.
- **No Chance of Counterfeit**
  Since the cryptocurrencies are digital and are constantly being created by miners, there is very little chance of them being counterfeited.
- **Instant Transactions**
  Transactions with cryptocurrencies are made within a matter of minutes as long as both parties have a quick internet connection. This is very convenient for buyers, sellers and traders.
- **Very Little Risk of Identity Theft**
  As previously stated, you don't have to send any information aside from the amount of money so there is minimal risk of having your identity stolen.
- **Available for Everyone**
  Anyone and everyone can start buying, using and transacting with cryptocurrencies. It depends on you if you would choose to enter the market and deal with cryptocurrency and everything it encompasses.
- **The Decentralization Feature**

Cryptocurrency is managed by a network of computers all around the world using blockchain technology. This means that any kind of government has no access to it.

- **Worldwide Recognition**
Cryptocurrency is not limited by any interest or exchange rates or transaction fees in any particular country. This means it can be used by anyone in the world smoothly and easily, saving the users lots of time, effort and money as well.

Although there are many advantages to using cryptocurrency, it still has a long way to go before it can and will be used in place of real money. Aside from the fact that a lot of people are still unaware about it, it is still unstable and limited.

But if the development of cryptocurrency continues as it does now, its future seems quite bright.

Are There Disadvantages Too?

Just like everything in this world, cryptocurrency comes with a list of disadvantages. In some cases, one or more of these become the determining factor whether a person would decide on investing in cryptocurrency.

In reality, a lot of people haven't even heard of cryptocurrency and it cannot spread and be used if they don't educate themselves all about it. Not only people, the majority of businesses have yet to accept it and use it in their trade for the word about it to spread.

It would be good to be informed of the different disadvantages of using this as it cen help you weigh your options and make a smart and informed decision which you won't end up regretting.

Here are the different disadvantages of cryptocurrency:

- **There is a Fairly High Risk of Loss**
  Just like any online transaction or online application, it comes with a high risk of loss. As the producers of cryptocurrency are trying to increase their security features, other nefarious people are also working on finding ways to get around the security.
  This is why people generally don't put too much of their money in cryptocurrency and when they do invest, they are very careful about keeping their information private to avoid being hacked and robbed from.
- **There is a Lack of Security**
  As a matter of fact, there is no seamless way to ensure the protection of cryptocurrency from human errors (such as using easy passwords to crack), technical problems (such as the occurrence of malware or hardware failure) or even fiduciary deception.
  These are the main reasons why many people claim that cryptocurrency doesn't have ample security.

- **There is a Chance of Heightened Regulation**

  Right now, cryptocurrency has simple and user friendly guidelines which are beneficial for all its users. However, there is a chance that the government or any other agencies in charge of law enforcement might see cryptocurrency as a way for money laundering to be done right out in public.

  If this happens, they might start to establish more strict regulations, which would lessen the number of users thus lowering the value of the currency.

- **It's Limited and Doesn't Have That Many Applications**

  The system of cryptocurrency was created in such a way that the speed and quantity of transactions which can be processed is limited. This means that there is a very low likelihood that it will be replacing credit and debit cards in the near future.

  While cryptocurrency is gaining popularity, there is a question on where you can actually make use of it, aside from using it to make illicit transactions. Cryptocurrency would have a better chance of flourishing and spreading to a larger population of users if it had more practical applications, such as for fundraising campaigns or international money tranfers.

- **It's Can be Quite Complicated**

As you can see, a lot of things are involved in cryptocurrency. It may be a simple concept but it doesn't only involve the currency itself.

You would have to do a lot of research and gather a lot of knowledge and information in order to fully understand it and invest in it with little doubt.

- **It's Relatively Unstable**

  The value and exchange rates of cryptocurrency varies greatly. This means that with each day you transact with cryptocurrency, the value of your money can be different. There is a chance that cryptocurrency market will stabilize, however, when that will happen is still unsure.

- **It's Novel and Hasn't Achieved Total General Awareness Yet**

  Yes, Bitcoin has become quite known and popular, however it would take more time for other kinds of cryptocurrencies to peak and gain as much users. Also, though a lot of people and businesses are beginning to gain awareness and acceptance in using cryptocurrency, the number of users is a lot less compared to those who use credit and debit cards.

These are a few of the most significant disadvantages of cryptocurrency. Knowing them is essential when you're thinking about getting into the whole market of cryptocurrency.

Cryptocurrency Myths and Misconceptions

As there are a lot of opinions about cryptocurrency out there on different sources, it could be quite overwhelming to pour through each abd every resource in order to find out which are fact and which are fiction. Just like any other trend that emerges in the world, cryptocurrency comes with its own myths and misconceptions which have very little truth in it.

If you are looking to start using cryptocurrencies, it would be beneficial to know these myths and misconceptions so that you cannot be easily disconcerted when you read or hear about them. These myths can appear in different articles or blogs and can lower the interest of anyone who would lke to start using cryptocurrency.

Here are the most common myths and misconceptions which give cryptocurrency a less than desirable image.

- **The Cryptocurrency Market is Finished**
  Though a lot of people are already making use of cryptocurrency, a lot of people are already proclaiming that the trend is fading and that less and less people are using it. Fact is, cryptocurrency, though relatively new, is beginning to gain momentum. A lot of kinds of cryptocurrencies are available in the market and as people are beginning to take notice, they become interested, they educate themselves and eventually join the cryptocurrency market.

Think about it, when the first car was invented and introduced to the world, people saw it as a hazardous death trap and that it could never be as efficient as the horse-drawn carriage. But look at it now - almost 90% of families and households in the United States alone have at least one car in their garage. They can be seen everywhere in the world and more and more models are being released with new features. In a similar way, cryptocurrency has the potential to change the whole course of commerce, banking and financial processes. It can potentially make transfer of currency simpler, quicker and more secure than how we have right now.

Of course, cryptocurrency still has a long way to go before it would be able to replace our traditional banks. Right now, the idea is still fairly new and the majority of the population is still unaware of its uses and benefits. But that doesn't mean that it's already out of the picture and it won't be able to grow and influence more people in the world.

- **Cryptocurrency is Only for Criminals and Shady Individuals**
  An understandable misconconception but totally untrue. Just because a lot of people say that only criminals and nefarious organizations use cryptocurrency to buy and sell drugs or perform illegal transactions on the darknet, doesn't make it a fact.

These damaging statements about cryptocurrency doesn't allow the people to see how it can potentially open up or digitally link financial markets all over the globe.

It is a fact that cryptocurrency is used to perform shady dealings, and yes, by criminals and people of the sort, but the majority of cryptocurrency users aren't bad. They actually see how easy and beneficial it is to use cryptocurrency and so they continue to use it for their financial transactions.

Let's look at another real case - that of the internet. When the internet emerged around the year 1991, people thought that it was mainly for the use of thieves and pornographers. But look at it now. Since it is an amazing and beneficial kind of technology which actually has more benefits than disadvantages, it has become part of our way of life, allowing us to communicate with each other better.

What once started out as a suspicious change actually turned out to be better for the world - and cryptocurrency may have a similar potential.

- **Cryptocurrency is Not Safe At All**
  Actually, if you do your research well and you learn how to use cryptocurrency properly, it can potentially be one of the safest forms of currency that you can make use of.
  Cryptocurrency transactions are very simple and easy, but keep in mind that one you have sent an amount of money, you cannot take it

back. Tht's how fast and efficient the process is. Transactions are made and completed within minutes so you have to be 100% sure before sending money.

The safety if your cryptocurrency wallet actually lies with you. Just like your real wallet where you keep all your cash, your cryptocurrency wallet comes with a key, which you can use for transactions. It is crucial to keep this key private and secure so as not to compromise your account. Just as you would keep your PIN or other banking information secure, so should you do with your private key/s.

There are different cryptocurrency wallet services available so find out which are the most reliable ones and you can go with those.

- **Cryptocurrency is Expensive**
Another myth which doesn't hold much truth. Aside from the fact that setting up an account with cryptocurrency is free, the few transaction fees are so small you might not even feel them.

- **Cryptocurrency is Basically Useless**
This is very far from the truth. Cryptocurrency can actually be used the same way as fiat currency, only without limits to where it can be used. You can make use of cryptocurrency anywhere in the world without having to exchange them to fit into the currency of the different countries.

You can actually use several kinds of cryptocurrency to make online purchases. A lot of companies have started accepting cryptocurrency as a method of payment and since it is new, they come with promotions and discounts to sweeten the deal.

The cryptocurrency market is also famous for its volatility, which gives experienced market investors opportunity to make money by monitoring the cryptocurrency market and taking advantage of those who tend to panic-sell whenever there is a drop in the market.

- **It is Dangerously Unstable**

  It is a known fact that the cryptocurrency market is unstable, but not dangerously so. There are times when the market drops, but it doesn't last. Another moment the market spikes again and those who have sold their cryptocurrency out of panic would have already lost their investment.

  As the years went by, though, the cryptocurrency market has constantly, though gradually, gone up, proving that its instability is not at all a danger.

- **Cryptocurrency Sites Could Get Shut Down**

  This is actually a valid concern for people - what would happen if the cryptocurrency site they have signed up with gets shut down, what happens to their money then?

  Well, cryptocurrency actually works in a different way. Since it operates using a blockchain and a network of users all around the world work together to keep cryptocurrency in operation, this means that there is no "off switch." If some users are somehow disconnected, there are other users from other countries who would still be working on producing and making transactions with cryptocurrency.

- **Cryptocurrency is Not Legitimate**
There are hundreds of kinds of cryptocurrencies out there in the market, some even discussed in this book. Yes, there may be some cryptocurrencies which are not legitimate out of the hundreds of kinds, but that would only mean that you should be very careful in selecting which one you will use.
Educate yourself on the different kinds of cryptocurrency before making an actual choice. Get as much information as you can, both good and bad about the different kinds to increase the chances that the one you pick is in fact, legit.

- **Cryptocurrency is Only for the Rich**
As previously stated, all you would need is a computer or device with acces to the internet and some money to purchase cryptocurrency. You don't have to be fabulously wealthy in order to sign up for and start using it. It is for everyone who is willing to take a chance on it.

There you have it, some of the most comon cryptocurrency myths which could discourage you from using them. If you happen to stumble upon more of these, it would be best to learn about the validity of the claim before believing it.

Some Advice for Beginners

Now that you're aware of the main advantages and disadvantages of cryptocurrency, you probably have a clearer picture of the benefits and risks of using it.

At this point, you have either become more reluctant to join the trend of cryptocurrency or you have become more interested in it. If you are part of the latter, then it would be more helpful for you to learn about some useful advice for cryptocurrency beginners.

The more information you have, the better chance you'd have of making smart decisions to be able to get the most out of your money. Unless you're a thrill seeker or a risk junkie, you'd probably benefit from a good set of advice which you may find useful in the long run.

1. **Disregard Sources of Information which are Biased**
   When doing research, look for sources which are reputable and don't advertise too much and seem inclined to convincing you to invest in just one particular cryptocurrency. Remember that there are a lot of scammers out there who put up sites just for the purpose of enticing newbies by using false information and radical advertising. More objective sources which are unbiased are probably more trustworthy as they give you all information about a certain product

- or a kind of cryptocurrency, including the negative points.

2. **Only Invest What You Can**

   It has been discussed earlier that it is absolutely not a good idea to invest everything you have into cryptocurrency. This goes for any kind of investment. It is always a better idea to start small and hope for the best. This way, if you earn money, then it's great! But if you happen to lose money, it shouldn't be the cause for you to drown in debt or lose all the money you have.

3. **Plan Goals which You Know You can Achieve**

   Keep in mind that cryptocurrency isn't a way for you to get rich in a short amount of time. Be realistic in setting your goals in regards to the returns of your investment in cryptocurrency. Also remember that the market of cryptocurrency is unstable so you may need to stick with it even if it goes down at times.

4. **Resist the Urge to Panic**

   Do your research before you begin and study the cryptocurrency market. Doing this can lessen your tendency to panic and make impulsive decisions in the future.

5. **Try to Make Smart Decisions**

   In dealing with cryptocurrency, or any other investment for that matter, you never try to guess what's going to happen next in the market. Investment markets are often unstable and you would have to think first and be smart before you make any decisions about your cryptocurrency. To be able to make smart decisions, you have to do your research and put in the work - observe the cryptocurrency market to be able to see its trends.

6. **Learn from Your Errors**

   It cannot be said enough - the cryptocurrency market is volatile and there may come a time when you end up making a bad decision with your cryptocurrency. When that happens, the mportant thing is not to give up. Instead, try to find out what went wrong and what had caused you to make that error. Learn from your errors to be able to move forward.

7. **Plan Out Your Strategies**

   Learn to follow the trends of the cryptocurrency market in order to understand them more. It would be useful to also learn how to interpret charts and be sure to keep track of your investment in real time. In doing this, you could be able to make plans on how you will carry out the next steps of your cryptocurrency investment.

8. **Don't Get Left Behind**

   In order to get the most out of your cryptocurrency, you have to educate yourself. The more you learn, the more you will know and the more you will be able to make the right choices when buying, selling, using or trading your cryptocurrency. As they say, knowledge is power so go ahead and get as much knowledge as you can.

These are simple yet useful advice and it would be your choice to follow them or find your own methods to succeed in the cryptocurrency game.

The Legitimacy of Cryptocurrency

When you think about it, just the name cryptocurrency suggests something cryptic or mysterious. Though growing in popularity, it still remains a mystery to a lot of people.

The core thought and main purpose of cryptocurrency was to have a quicker and cheaper method or moving funds on a global scale, without having to deal with banks or the government. Because of this, it has gained a lot of momentum from users who valued privacy and anonymity, though some of those users had less than noble reasons of their own.

But really, how legitimate is cryptocurrency and how safe is it to use?

Cryptocurrency has already been around for a few years, but it is still considered to be in the earlier stages of its development. There are many opinions regarding the legitimacy of cryptocurrency though most of them are baseless.

It would be quite difficult to actually answer the question of the legitimacy of cryptocurrency. Since a lot of users are able to successfully use and transact with cryptocurrency, you'd think that would be enough to consider it as legit. However, as it is decentralized by nature and it cannot be controlled by the government, then maybe it cannot be considered as legit.

Probably the best thing you can do is learn how to spot scams around cryptocurrency and how to protect yourself from them and take precautionary security measures.

How to Spot Cryptocurrency Scams

To be able to identify cryptocurrency scams, you'd have to be vigilant and aware of the warning signs. A lot of scams carry the same warning signs, making it a bit easier for you to spot them.

In looking for the perfect cryptocurrency to use, you would have to be aware of these points so that you won't fall into the hands of scammers who are just interested in getting your money.

- **You are Given an Opportunity to "Get Rich Quick!"**
  Think about it, why would a total stranger help you get rich quick out of the blue? If you are presented with a chance to make a lot of money in a short amount of time, this is probably a scam. As what has been mentioned over and over again, cryptocurrency is in no way a get-rich-quick scheme so if you encounter something like this, just ignore it and move on.
- **The Offer Seems Too Good to be True**

When it comes to investing in cryptocurrency, if the offer seems too good to be true, it probably is. Offers which present returns which are double or triple the amount of your money are most likely just scams. Dealing with cryptocurrency takes a lot of time, effort and smart decision making, not just fast deals which are filled with empty promises.

- **You Cannot Confirm What is Being Claimed**
  When you are given an offer or when you see an interesting kind of cryptocurrency wherein someone is communicating with you about all the benefits of signing up, do more research and see if you can confirm or verify what is being claimed. "Hidden" or "stealth" offers make no sense and are most likely scams.

- **The Most Basic Data is Missing**
  In your search for the cryptocurrency which you will use, be mindful of all the information about the company or organization you plan to sign up with. Research the roots and history of the corporation which owns the cryptocurrency especially if it's new or it isn't that popular. If you notice that basic data- such as the owners of the company or the physical address of the office, are missing, it would be better to move on to more concrete options.

- **Base of Operations in Another Country**
  If they claim that the main office or base of operations of the company is in a different country, be wary. It might happen to be in a

country with very little regard for the law or a country which, conveniently, speaks a different language, one which you don't understand - making it difficult for you to estabilsh good communication with them if any issues arise.

- **Too Much False and "Good" Advertising**
If the company which owns the cryptocurrency gives out too much information on how gallant and righteous they are, how they are only working towards selfless deeds and how enormous profits come as merely a bonus, it would be wise not to just jump on the wagon and invest everything you have. Again, do more research as things like this are most likely just a scam.

- **You are Offered Higher Returns if you Invest More Initally**
Often a mistake made by beginners, they are dazzled with offers of bigger profits, the more money they put in as they sign up. This is just not true. Scammers are able to entice newbies with offers like this before disappearing once the big amount og money has already been given to them.

- **You are Given a Compensation Plan**
This only works for salespeople who have to meet quotas in order to get higher commisions. This kind of strategy doesn't apply to investors so you won't be needing a compensation plan when you buy, use, trade or sell cryptocurrency as you'd just be using it for transactions to either send or receive money.

- **You'd Have to Recruit More Investors to Earn**
  This is not how cryptocurrency works. In fact, one of the features is you will be able to enjoy your anonymity so if you are asked to recruit others, this is nothing but a scam.
- **There is No Concrete Product**
  Of course you'd have to be able to see your money as cryptocurrency. Without it, you have nothing to show for your investment.
- **All the Information About the Cryptocurrency is Unclear**
  By now you have a lotmore information about cryptocurrency. If in your search to find the one you will invest in you encounter one which gives vague or unclear information, there's a very high likelihood that it's not real.
- **You Cannot Exchange Your Cryptocurrency**
  You have to be able to exchange your cryptocurrency for fiat currency otherwise it would have no value. So make sure that you have this option before making an investment.

Since cryptocurrency is digital, that makes it easy for people with the right skills to simulate a kind of cryptocurrency along with a website where you can sign up for it. If you're not careful, you may be tricked into signing up on a site for a cryptocurrency that doesn't actually exist!

To avoid this, remember to be wary of signing up. Do your research and make sure the cryptocurrency exists and you will be able to use it.

Safety Tips in Using Cryptocurrency

Being able to spot scams is pertinent when dealing with cryptocurrency so you don't end up losing money at the very beginning, before you even start using it. To improve on that, you could also benefit from safety tips in using cryptocurrency.

When you use these tips along with being aware of the scams and scammers which can entrap you, you may have an easier time joining the cryptocurrency market. Once in, you'd have to maintain your safety also by using some of the tips in this list.

These safety tips are designed to help you efficiently make use of your cryptocurrency so you can get the most out of it.

1. Use Different Wallets for Your Cryptocurrency

Since transactions are fast and easy, you can create multiple wallets for different purposes. Make separate wallets for cryptocurrency which you plan to send, cryptocurrency which you plan to save or cryptocurrency which you receive.

Since there is no limit to the number or wallets a person can own, take advantage of that and divide your cryptocurrency. If you do this, there would be a lesser chance of your cryptocurrency being compromised.

2. Never Use Web Wallets for Your Savings

Web wallets are prone to hacking and there have been recent cases wherein they have been compromised and robbed of all their contents. Yes, they are convenient, but keeping your savings in them might not be the smartest choice. You can make use of web wallets for sending and receiving payments to enjoy their convenience while still trying to be safe.

3. Secure Your Identity

Never, EVER share your private keys to anyone. It would be like giving away the PIN to your ATM card. If you share this information to anyone, you are placing your identity and your privacy in danger. It would make gaining access to your account a lot easier for the wrong sort of people.

4. Go Offline

Keeping your cryptocurrency in a wallet which is stored in your computer would make you quite prone to attacks from hackers or viruses. To augment your security, you can keep your private key in an offline location like in a flashdisk or written on a piece of paper. To gain access to your wallet, you'd have to manually enter your private key, which would take longer but if it would keep your cryptocurrency safe, why not?

5. Realize the Relevance of Backing Up

To be able to save all the information related to your cryptocurrency, you can back everything up on an external hard drive or flashdisk. You can also encrypt your data if you know how to keep it private even if someone obtains your backup files somehow.

Taking these precautionary measures may be able to help you secure your cryptocurrency account, allowing you to freely conduct transactions and get the most out of your currency.

Cryptocurrency Highlight: Bitcoin

One of the most popular and most widely used kinds of cryptocurrency is Bitcoin. Even if you haven't started using cryptocurrency, you would have most likely heard of Bitcoin already. Just like any other cryptocurrency, Bitcoin is made and used digitally or electronically.

Bitcoin isn't controlled by anyone specific and this kind of currency isn't concretely printed like other fiat currencies. Instead, they are made by people and, more recently, businesses which are operating on computers all over the world. Bitcoins are made with the use of a software which analyzes and solves mathematical equations.

As this is the most popular cryptocurrency in the world right now, let's take a closer look at Bitcoins. This will help you get a better understanding of cryptocurrency as you would be learning about a specific kind of cryptocurrency which is familiar to all cryptocurrency users.

All About Bitcoins

Bitcoin was the very first kind of cryptocurrency which had emerged in the world and it is still around until these recent times. It was created by Satoshi

Nakamoto, who was a developer of software. He proposed Bitcoin to be an electronic or digital currency system for transactions which would be based on mathematical proof.

Satoshi's idea was to come up with a form of currency which would be separate from any central authority. He also conceptualized that Bitcoin would be electronically transferable in an instant and users won't have to deal with pricey fees for transactions.

Though regular or traditional currency somehow originated from gold and silver, cryptocurrency has a totally different basis. For fiat currency, if you give money to the bank, at some point you can get it back. It's concrete and can be physically passed on from person to person. Bitcoin, however, is nothing like that. It is actually based on mathematics and mathematical verification.

All around the globe, users utilize software programs which are based on mathematical formulas in order to create Bitcoins. These formulas or equations are available to anyone so technically anyone can use or produce it. As it is open for anyone, it means that everyone can view it to monitor the progress of production and transactions.

As you may know by now, Bitcoins are radically different from traditional currency. Let's look at the different characteristics of Bitcoins which set them apart from regular money.

In fact, some, if not most of these characteristics are similar across all other kinds of cryptocurrency. These relevant features are only applicable to Bitcoin and possibly to other kinds of cryptocurrency but not to fiat currency.

- **Bitcoin is Decentralized**
  The Bitcoin network is not controlled by one single person or one single organization. Each and every user on a computer who mines bitcoins and processes different transactions contribute to the whole network as they all work together.
  Theoretically, therefore, no one person or organization has the ability to interfere with any policies concering the currency, which could cause a meltdown. Also, no one has the authority to just seize the bitcoins of a user or freeze a user's account. Finally, even if one or more parts of the network loses their connection or goes offline, the processes don't discontinue so the currency just continues to flow.
- **Bitcoin Set-Up is Very Simple**
  At times, signing on with traditional banks can be quite complicated and challenging, especially since they ask for so many requirements when you are to open an account. To be able to set-up an account (or address) with Bitcoin, you would only need a few seconds to a few minutes, depending on the speed of your internet connection. You won't be

asked any questions and you won't have to pay
any fees.

- **Bitcoin Ensures Your Privacy**
There is a level of privacy that comes with
signing up with Bitcoin. Your personal
information doesn't have to be given when you
sign up with Bitcoin or when you do any
transaction. You can have more that one bitcoin
addresses which won't be linked to any of your
personal information.

- **Bitcoin Offers Tranparency to All Its
Users**
Bitcoin has a master ledger, called the
blockchain, that records each and every
transaction which transpired in the Bitcoin
network and everyone has access to it.
If you happen to have a bitcoin address which is
used publicly, anyone will be able to see the
amount of bitcoins you have in the said
address. However, they wouldn't know who
actually owns it.
Because of this, some users then make use of
multiple bitcoin addresses and never place big
quantities of bitcoins in just one address.

- **Bitcoin Has Very Minimal Transaction
Fees**
Whatever fees Bitcoin would charge to you are
very minimal and you might not even notice
them, unlike when you have an international
money transfer at your bank. You'd either have
to pay a fixed fee or you'd have to pay a fee

depending on the amount you transfer, which can be inconvenient.

- **Bitcoin's Processes are Lightning Quick**
  As long as you have a very good internet connection, you will be able to send to and receive money from anywhere and be sure that the transaction is completed within minutes. As soon as the Bitcoin network processes the transaction, it immediately goes through.
- **Bitcoin Processes Cannot Be Reversed**
  As soon as you send bitcoins and they are processed and verified by the network, you cannot get them back anymore - unless the one who received the bitcoins sends them back to you.

As you can see, Bitcoin really is different from regular currency. These characteristics set it apart from fiat currency as a newer and more innovative way of transacting funds.

Advantages of Using Bitcoin

You now know more about Bitcoin and the currency that comes with it. It has been around since 2009, and for good reason. Using Bitcoin comes with a number of advantages, aside from the fact that it is the most long-standing kind of currency available today.

Transactions in Bitcoin are made through a huge network of users all around the globe who are all connected by a shared program. These transactions are then recorded in the blockchain, which can be accessed by all users in the network. Bitcoins can either be mined by soling difficult mathematical equations or bought using fiat currency and stored in your bitcoin wallet.

If you're trying to find the right cryptocurrency to start using, maybe Bitcoin is the one. Here are the advantages of using Bitcoin to help inform you and possibly guide you in making your choice.

1. Protected User Identity

Whether you sign up or make transactions on Bitcoin, you won't have to give out any personal information, which can be dangerous especially when it comes to online processing. Though all transactions or public bitcoin addresses can be found in the blockchain, none of the users will be able to link them to you as a user. Also, the address which is created for purchases changes with each and every transaction.

2. Uninterrupted Service

Banks, financial institions, law enforcement agencies or the government cannot interfere with you Bitcoin account or with any of your transactions. This gives you more freedom to manage your currency and transact in the network.

3. Taxes Do Not Apply

Since the government (or basically any third party) has no ware of discovering, monitoring or interrupting your transactions, no sales taxes are added to any of the items or bitcoins you purchase. This saves you a lot of money as compared to purchasing with traditional currency.

4. Minimal Transaction Fees

While foreign purchases and standard wire transfers usually come with charges and currency exchange fees, Bitcoin doesn't. There are some transaction fees, but they are so small they are negligible.

5. Flexible Transactions

Since transactions with Bitcoin are done online, you can perform them on your computer or on any of your devices which are connected to the internet, even your mobile phone! You won't have to go to the store or to a bank to purchase and make payments for items. All you need is to go online and start making your payments or other transactions.

Yes, using Bitcoin does have a number of advantages so it's up to you if these advantages are enough to convince you to start using Bitcoin.

Other Alternatives to Bitcoin

Still not convinced enough to use Bitcoin? You don't have to. An important thing to keep in mind is that when you do finally make a decision to use cryptocurrency and you choose which kind to go with, you should be happy with your choice at the end of the day. Then you won't have to deal with and maintain something which you weren't really sure you wanted from the very beginning.

Doing this wouldn't allow you to effectively manage your cryptocurrency, so don't do it! Fortunately, Bitcoin isn't the only kind of cryptocurrency available out there. Yes, it was the very first so actually it also acted as sort of a trendsetter, which allowed for a variety of other cryptocurrencies to appear, all built on a P2P network which is decentralized. Bitcoin has also acted as the base standard for all other cryptocurrencies.

These other cryptocurrencies (also known as Altcoins) are basically just altered, revised or even improved versions of Bitcoin. Let's take a look at the best alternative kinds of cryptocurrency to Bitcoin out there and learn more about them.

- **Litecoin (LTC)**
  Created by Charle Lee, a former Google engineer who also happens to be a graduate of MIT, and was launched in 2011. Litecoin is similar to Bitcoin in a lot of ways but it has an added advantage of faster transaction verification. This is made possible by its speedier rate of block generation. This could be a good substitute for Bitcoin if it isn't really for you.
- **Ethereum (ETH)**

This cryptocurrency was launched in 2015, which makes it one of the newer options. Ethereum's software platform is able to avoid fraud, unwanted control, disruption from a third party or even any downtime while building and running Distributed Applications or Smart Contracts.

Applications on this kind of cryptocurrency operate on ether, which is its platform-specific cryptographic token. It can be compared with a vehicle which can be used to move around the Ethereum platform.

The creators of Ethereum have stated that it can be used to secure, decentralize, trade and codify just about anything.

- **Zcash (ZEC)**

  This cryptocurrency was released late in 2016, making it a lot newer than Ethereum but it shows a lot of promise. Zcash has a new privacy feature which allows users to select the transparency of their transactions. Unlike in Bitcoin, where all transactions can be viewed by everyone involved, Zcash allos users to "shield" some of their transactions through an advanced cryptographic method called zk-SNARK, which they had developed.

- **Dash**

  Launched in 2014 and was originally known by the name Darkcoin, this is a more secretive or discreet version of Bitcoin. Dash provides more anonymity for its users since it operates on a mastercode network which is also decentralized, making transactions next to untraceable.

- **Monero (XMR)**

  Monero is a private, very secure and impossible to trace kind of currency which was launched early in 2014. After a short while it had already grown as in called the attention and interest of the cryptography community and the cryptography enthusiasts. It is known as an open source cryptocurrency as its development is based on donations and is driven by its community of users. Monero has different features from Bitcoin, which is why users have chosen it over the more popular choice.

Final Words on Cryptocurrency

Thre you have it - an extensive and comprehensive summary of everything you need to know about cryptocurrency. Just like everything in this world, it comes with a lot of good points and some bad points as well. All you have to do is weigh your options and check whether you'd be willing to deal with the negatives to be able to enjoy the positives.

But in reality, what is the future of cryptocurrency? Would it endure for years and years more or is the trend about to end sooner rather than later?

We know as a fact the the cryptocurrency market is unpredictable and fast. As fast as the days go by, new kinds of cryptocurrencies are created, older ones fade away, pioneers earn a lot from their investments while other investors actually end up losing their money. Each and every type of cryptocurrency which emerge come with a promise of a lot of benefits along with a story of how it came to be in order to grab the attention of potential users.

While some kinds endure and have been around for a good number of years with no sign of stopping, a lot of them last for only a few months and carry on as long as they still have coins or until the investors lose everything they put in.

The way things are going now, though, it seems like cryptocurrencies are here to stay and to influence change in the world. Cryptocurrencies are gradually - and consistently, gaining popularity as more people are gaining awareness, getting educated and finally joining the market.

It almost seems like a revolution as more people and businesses are accepting cryptocurrency as a means of transferring money anywhere in the world. Now the question remains - will you join the market too?

Thanks again for taking the time to read this book!

You should now have a good understanding of Cryptocurrenies, and be able to analyse the Cryptocurrency market to buy your own!

If you enjoyed this book, please take the time to leave me a review on Amazon. I appreciate your honest feedback, and it really helps me to continue producing high quality books.

51703342R00048

Made in the USA
San Bernardino, CA
29 July 2017